The Gorgeous COLORING BOOK FOR GROWN-UPS

METRO BOOKS
New York

METRO BOOKS
New York

An Imprint of Sterling Publishing
1166 Avenue of the Americas
New York, NY 10036

Designed by Ana Bjezancevic

Illustrations by Shutterstock.com

ISBN 978-1-4351-6179-5

For information about custom editions, special sales, and premium
and corporate purchases, please contact Sterling Special Sales
at 800-805-5489 or specialsales@sterlingpublishing.com.

Manufactured in China

2 4 6 8 10 9 7 5 3

www.sterlingpublishing.com

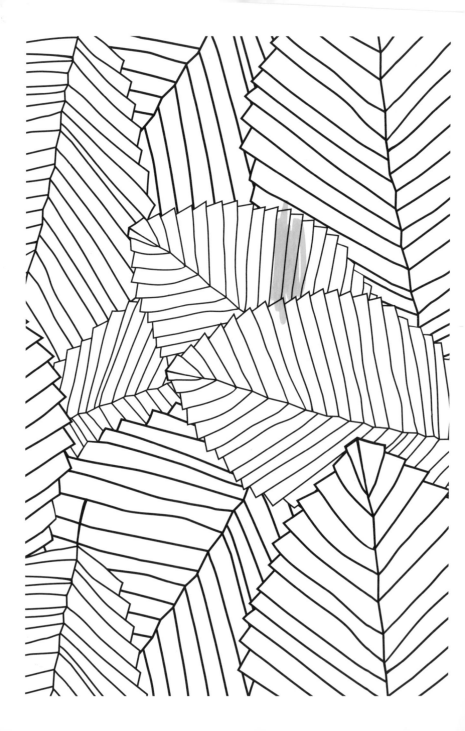

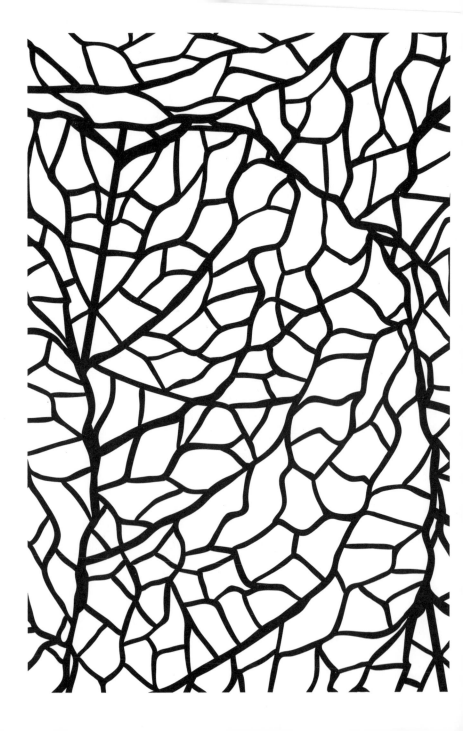

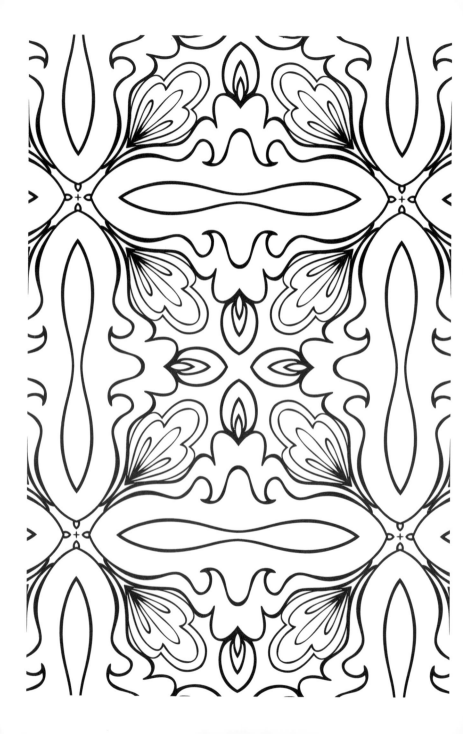

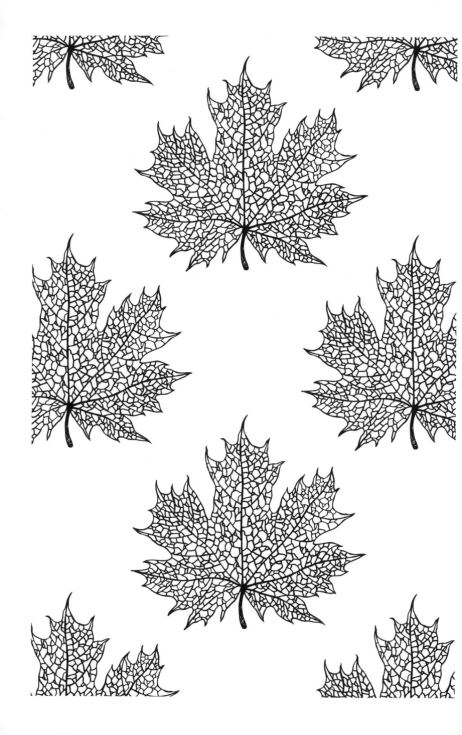